Disclaimer

The information provided herein is stated to be truthful and consistent, in that any liability, in terms of inattention or otherwise, by any usage or abuse of any policies, processes, or directions contained within is the solitary and utter responsibility of the recipient reader.

The information herein is offered for informational purposes solely, and is universal as so. The presentation of the information is without contract or any type of guarantee assurance.

Under no circumstances will any legal responsibility or blame be held against the author or publisher for any reparation, damages, or monetary loss due to the information herein, either directly or indirectly.

Before Getting Started

First and foremost thank you for downloading my cookbook. Many well-established kitchen gurus have helped with crafting these unique recipes and without their contributions this would not be possible. I sincerely hope you enjoy it.

Also, if you would be kind enough to leave a positive review on Amazon it would be greatly appreciated. You have no idea how much it helps us independent authors!

Your friend,
Carla

Table of Contents

Sage & Onion Bread
Moravian Sugar Cake
Cheddar Bread
Sweet Hawaiian Yeast Bread
Multigrain Health Bread
Tomato Bread
Cinnabuns
Pumpernickel
Russian Black Bread
Banana Nut Bread
Classic Hamburger Buns
Sweet Cinnamon Bread
Pita Bread
Caramelized Onion Focaccia
100% Whole Wheat Brown Bread
Brioche
Italian Country Bread
Stuffed Focaccia
Sour Cream Chive Bread
Basic Dinner Rolls
The Herb Garden Bread
Beetroot Bread
Hoagie Rolls

Introduction

What is a Bread Machine?

People love bread. They will do anything to get their hands on a wholesome loaf of happiness. History tells us that the Ancient Egyptians used bread as currency, it was so important. So in our hurried age, it's no surprise that the need for tasty, artisan-made bread was cross-"bread" with automated efficiency. Henceforth spawned... the bread machine!

The History of Bread Machines

These machines have been around since the early 1900's in various forms but only became available for domestic use in the 1980's, thanks to the Japanese company we now know as Panasonic. Naturally, there have been many improvements over time and said machines can now whip up all sorts of tasty treats, ranging from popcorn to jellies to chocolate cake (and bread, of course).

Tips for Using Bread Machines

So, what's the big deal about a bread machine then?

Well, it's a machine. We love gadgets and gizmos with magical abilities. What could be nicer than dumping a bunch of ingredients into a metal tub, pushing a few buttons before retiring for the night, and then waking to the smell of fresh, bready goodness? The medical field has yet to identify the fear of dough as an actual phobia, but all that you need to do to bake your very own amazing bread is pour a pre-mix into the pan, push a button and run away. Problem solved.

On a less terrifying note, most of us are simply intimidated by the leavening process and the seemingly inevitable outcome involving a bread-like brick, a hacksaw and a visit to the dentist. Having a machine do all the dirty work for you is quite a blessing... and if the bread fails – blame the machine!

If, however, your machine consistently bakes inedible rocks for you, fear not. You can affect the outcome of your loaf more than you think. Because a bread machine is a relatively simple device, it doesn't "look" at the dough to see if it is rising too fast or slow. If the room is too cold, it may not be able to compensate and the yeast will develop too slowly. This may mean your bread is going to be baked prematurely. If you can't move to a warmer spot, try putting a little jug of water in the microwave for 5 minutes on high before popping the bread pan inside (be careful not to start the microwave with the bread pan in it!!). Bread loves a good sauna.

Buy yourself an instant-read thermometer, like the kind you use to test a roast for doneness. Seriously. Bread machines are robotic and bake until the program is done. So if the bread has been smelling cooked for ages but still has 20 minutes to go, open the lid quickly and check the center (mind not to measure too close to any metal parts). Bread is cooked at 190°F exactly.

Something to keep in mind is that all yeasts and flours are created equal.

Good quality flour can be a bit on the pricey side, but is well worth it. Bread flour is more glutinous (sticky) than good ol' cake flour. Then there are the whole wheat and alternative grain flours. These take longer to rise and can be tricky for a first time bread-maker. Keep a close eye on the dough the first time you try them.

Yeasts are a topic for an article of their very own, but here's the skinny. There are two kinds of yeast you need to know about: bread machine/instant/rapid rising yeast and active dry yeast. Mostly, they are interchangeable (think tortoise vs hare), but recipes will usually stipulate which is better for that particular bread. By way of example, brown bread needs to do a "slow and steady" race to the finish, so using a fast-rise yeast may cause it to collapse in exhaustion, leaving you with a tasty, but sad loaf of bread.

Many folks who love their bread machines still swear by a traditional oven for the baking portion of the deal. Kneading and shaping dough can be a messy business, so before you work with it, grease your hands lightly, work lightly, hum softly. Talking to the dough also helps ease the tension some days.

The bottom line, really, is knowing your particular machine and figuring out what works for you. Remember, good bread takes patience and practice, no matter what method you use to construct it. If you struggle, there are some amazing blogs out there that can give you extra tips, pictures, and advice along the way.

People have been baking bread for centuries (pita bread has been said to date back 12,000 years), so someone, somewhere will be able to give you a hand in the greatest art (since sliced bread).

Recipes

Flax Seed Bread

This is not a grain–free recipe, but does include flax seed meal. Grind your flax seeds in a coffee grinder, a little at a time. Keep ground/whole flax seeds in the fridge as they are inclined to go rancid. Test before baking: if your flax is bitter, throw it out.

Serves: 18
Time to Prepare: 15 min

Ingredients

- ¼ oz Active Dry Yeast (1 package)
- 1¼ cups Lukewarm Water
- 3 Tbsp Organic Honey
- 1 Tbsp Oil (Olive works just fine)
- ½ Tsp Salt
- 1½ cups Whole Wheat or White Flour
- 1½ cups White Bread Flour
- Cornmeal for Dusting
- Poppy Seeds or Something Pretty to Stick to the Egg–wash
- Egg–wash Before Baking: 1 Egg, Lightly Mixed with 1 Tbsp Cold Water
- ⅔ cup Flax Seeds Ground to Make 1 cup of Flax Meal. Freshly Ground is Usually Tastier Than Commercially Pre–ground Flax Meal.

Directions

Pop the ingredients (except the cornmeal, egg wash, & poppy seeds) into the bread machine as directed by the manufacturer & set the cycle to "dough". Check the mix after 5–10 minutes & add a Tbsp of water or flour to adjust the consistency if needed.

When the dough is done, turn it out & shape into a loaf – round, square, oblong – & leave it to rise in a cornmeal–dusted baking pan of the appropriate shape.

Heat the oven to 400°F

Make a few diagonal slashes on the loaf top with a sharp knife (blunt or only partially sharp will just make a mess). Pop them in the oven for 15 minutes, lower the temp down to 350°F & bake for another 25 min. If you have a meat thermometer, it should read about 205°F when the bread is done. Turn the bread out onto a rack to cool for about 20 min before slicing.

Zucchini Herb Bread

Tired of the usual concoctions? Give this one a try & add it to your collection of whole wheat masterpieces.

Serves: 8
Time to Prepare: 15 min

Ingredients

- ¾ cup Lukewarm Water
- 1 Tbsp Raw Honey
- 1½ Tbsp Vegetable Oil
- 1 cup Grated Zucchini
- 1 cup Whole Wheat Flour
- 2½ cups Bread Flour
- ½ Tsp Dried Basil/Rosemary/Fresh Basil
- 1 Tbsp Sesame Seeds
- 1 Tsp Salt
- 2 Tsp Dry Active Yeast

Directions

Add the ingredients to your bread pan using the order recommended by the manufacturer. Set to whole wheat, light crust & press start to begin the magic.

Remember to leave the loaf to firm up/cool completely before slicing it.

Enjoy!

Marmalade Oat Bread

So if you can put cheese inside the bread instead of on it, why not make your toast & orange marmalade breakfast all in one meal? Much more efficient, don't you think?

Serves: 12
Time to Prepare: 5 min

Ingredients

- 1 cup & 2 Tbsp Warmed (But not hot) Milk
- 1½ Tsp Softened Butter
- 3¼ cups Bread Flour
- 1 Tsp Salt
- ¾ cup Rolled Oats
- 2 Tsp Yeast
- ½ cup Orange Marmalade (Lemon or grapefruit will do, but will yield a different flavor)

Directions

Measure out the ingredients into your bread pan in the order recommended by the manufacturer.

Get the machine going on the basic or white bread setting, & then sit back & wait for bread to magically appear for dinner.

Jalapeño Cheese Bread

Use of the time delay with this recipe is at your own discretion, but not generally recommended for recipes using cream & eggs

Serves: 6
Time to Prepare: 10 min

Ingredients

- ½ cup Sour Cream
- ⅛ cup Lukewarm Water
- 1 Lightly Beaten Egg
- 2 cups Flour (All–purpose)
- 1 Tsp Salt
- 1½ Tbsp Sugar
- ¼ Tsp Baking Soda
- ¾ cup Grated Cheddar Cheese
- 1½ Tsp Dry Active Yeast
- ± 3 Fresh Jalapeño Peppers (Seeds removed & finely chopped) or 2 Tbsp Diced Canned Peppers

Directions

Refer to the user guide for you bread machine & layer the ingredients listed here accordingly. Select a basic bread setting with a light crust.

When the bake cycle is complete, turn the bread out onto a cooling rack. Leave it to cool for an hour before slicing. Well, you can tuck right in if you really cannot restrain yourself… but it will be really hard to cut without squishing the loaf beyond recognition.

Pandesal Bread Rolls

This Filipino specialty is a dinner roll eaten at any time of day, or all day. Try this recipe out & enjoy the amazing flavor. You will make it again & again!

Serves: 24
Time to Prepare: 20 min

Ingredients

- ½ cup Water (Room temp)
- ¼ cup Evaporated Milk
- ½ cup Whole Milk (Room temp)
- 1 Lightly Mixed Egg (Room temp)
- ½ cup Table Sugar
- ¾ Tsp Salt
- 5 Tbsp Softened Butter/Marg
- 1 Tbsp Vegetable Oil
- 4 cups White Flour
- 3 Tsp Dry Active Yeast
- Breadcrumbs for Rolling the Bread Balls in

Directions

If the liquids are a little too cold, mix them together in a microwavable bowl & heat for 30sec or so.

Layer all the ingredients (except the breadcrumbs) as directed by the manufacturer, & start the dough cycle. Don't worry if it turns out a little sticky, this is ok.

When the dough is ready, scoop out balls of dough (roughly an ice–cream scoop size) & roll them in the breadcrumbs, pressing down lightly to make an oval shape.

Place on a prepared cookie sheet, cover & leave to rise in a cozy place until doubled in volume.

Heat the oven to 375°F & bake until golden brown (10–15 min).

Cheese & Pepperoni Bread

Make this one fresh. Use of the time delay feature on your machine is not recommended because of the pepperoni & cheese.

Serves: 8
Time to Prepare: 10 min

Ingredients

- 1 cup (+ 2 Tbsp if needed) Lukewarm Warm Water
- ⅓ cup Grated Mozzarella Cheese
- 2 Tbsp Sugar
- 1 ½ Tsp Garlic Salt
- 3 ¼ cups White Bread Flour
- 1½ Tsp Dry Active Yeast
- ⅔ cup Finely Chopped Up Pepperoni
- 1½ Tsp Dried Oregano (Roughly double amount if using freshly chopped oregano)

Directions

Layer the ingredients (except the pepperoni) as directed by the manufacturer of your machine.

Select a basic bread setting & pick a medium–light crust for a 1½ lb loaf. When the machine beeps, add the pepperoni.

Wait until the bread has cooled before slicing it.

Garlic Cheese Rolls

These rolls are a perfect dinner accompaniment. There's no rule stating you can't eat them for breakfast, mind you.

Serves: 12
Time to Prepare: 20 min

Ingredients

- 1 cup Warm Water
- 3 cups White Bread Flour
- 1½ Tsp Salt
- 1½ Tbsp Softened (But not melted) Butter
- 3 Tbsp Sugar
- 2 Tbsp Milk Powder
- 2 Tsp Dry Active Yeast
- ¼ cup Melted Butter
- 1 Crushed Clove of Garlic
- 2 Tbsp (More–or–less) Freshly Grated Parmesan Cheese

Directions

Layer all the ingredients (except the last 3: ¼ cup melted butter, garlic & parmesan) in the bread machine as per manufacturer's instructions & get it going on the dough cycle.

Prepare a clean, dry, lightly floured work surface. Turn the dough out, gently roll & stretch it into a 24"–long rope.

Get your cookie sheets (13x9") greased & ready.

Grab the sharpest knife you have in your house – except dad's Leatherman – & divide the rope in half, the two resulting pieces each in half again, aaaand one more time (you should have 8 equal portions). Divide each of these smaller portions into 3 segments. You should now have 24 pieces to shape into balls & pop onto the cookie sheet.

Mix the melted butter with the garlic & splash it over the balls, then sprinkle with the cheese. Leave to rise quietly somewhere until doubled. This may take anywhere from 30 min to an hour depending on ambient temperature, altitude, humidity & the color of your socks.

Get your oven to 375°. Bake until golden brown (10–15min).

Slice them open & serve warm.

Yum.

Cinnamon Raisin Bagels

This recipe can be transformed to be egg-free by omitting the egg wash & giving the bagels a quick spray with non-stick spray

Serves: 10
Time to Prepare: 1 hr 30 min

Ingredients

- ½ cup Raisins
- 1 Tbsp Ground Cinnamon
- 1 Tbsp Sugar
- 1 ¼ cups Warm (Not hot) Water
- 3 cups Bread Flour
- 3⅓ Tbsp Organic Brown Sugar
- 1 Tsp Salt
- 2½ Tsp Instant/Rapid Rise Yeast (or 3¼ Tsp dry active yeast)
- Sugar Water (3 qt water with 1 Tbsp sugar)
- Egg Wash (1 egg mixed with 1 Tbsp water)

Directions

Soak the raisins in some hot water for about 10 minutes so that they plump out a bit, then drain & pat them with a clean tea towel to lightly dry them. Mix them in with the cinnamon & sugar.

Pop all the other ingredients (except the egg wash & sugar water) into the bread pan as per manufacturer instructions. Set to "dough" & wait for the beep & toss in the cinnamon-raisin mix (you can put them in right away instead).

Remove the dough from the machine just before the first rise (roughly 20–30 min into the cycle) & turn it out onto a lightly floured workspace. Divide the lump into 8 equal balls but keep a two little bitty sample balls aside (for checking the dough just now). Push your thumb through the center of the big ball while you stretch the dough to form a bagel shape. Go slowly & patiently.

Set them (including the two test balls) to rise in a warm spot, covered.

Get your oven heating to 400°F so long.

Bring the sugar water to the boil. When you think the bagels have risen sufficiently, locate the little ball you reserved & drop it into the boiling water. If it floats immediately it is not a witch (apologies to Mr. M Python) & is ready to cook. This is called the drop test.

Lower your bagels into the water with a slotted spoon & let them boil 1½ min/side. Now pop them on a rack for a moment before brushing them with egg wash.

Transfer them to a greased cookie sheet & slip them into your oven for 15 min. Let them cool a bit after baking before tucking in. Enjoy.

Pull-Apart Bread

This is a favorite among many, especially children. Sweet cinnamon bread with a healthy dose of whole wheat.

Serves: 12
Time to Prepare: 10 min

Ingredients

- 1½ Tsp Active Dry Yeast
- 1¼ cups Bread Flour
- 1 cup Whole Wheat Flour
- 3 Tbsp Sugar
- ½ Tsp Salt
- 2 Tbsp Butter/Marg
- 2 Eggs Mixed Lightly with a Fork
- ½ cup Tepid Water
- 6 Tbsp Soft Butter for Greasing, Glazing Etc
- ½ cup Organic Brown Sugar
- 1 Tsp Ground Cinnamon

Directions

Check the user guide for your bread machine & layer the ingredients in the pan as directed. Get the machine going on the dough cycle.

Grease a tube/bundt pan with 2 Tbsp of soft butter & then sprinkle 2 Tbsp of sugar over the butter.

Mix the remaining sugar with the cinnamon & put in a little dish. Set aside. Melt the remaining 4 Tbsp of butter & set aside.

When ready, divide the dough into 12 portions & roll them first in the butter & then cinnamon sugar. Stuff them into the pan in layers & then leave to double in a warm spot.

Heat the oven to 350°F & bake for 25–30 minutes. As soon as it is baked, turn it out of the pan & leave to cool.

Soft Pretzels

Remarkably fun to make & fun to eat. Random trivia: Pretzels originated in Europe, most likely from the monks in the Early Middle Ages

Serves: 4
Time to Prepare: 2 hrs

Ingredients

The Dough:

- 1 x ¼ oz Envelope of Dry Active Yeast
- 1 Tbsp Sugar
- 3 cups Flour
- 1 cup Warm Water
- ½ Tsp Salt
- 2 Tbsp Oil
- Water Dip
- 2qt Boiling Water
- ⅛ cup Baking Soda
- 1 Lightly Whisked Egg White for Brushing After Dipping

Garnishing Suggestions:

- Coarse Salt
- Poppy or Sesame Seeds
- Melted Butter
- Cinnamon Sugar

Directions

Layer the dough ingredients in the bread pan as directed by the manufacturer & select the setting for white bread.

Remove the dough after the second rising cycle (most machines will beep at this point – but know your machine). Turn it out onto a lightly dusted work surface & divide in four. Divide each of these quarters into 3 pieces (you now have 12 bits in total).

Roll each bit out into a rope about 18" long. Bring the ends around & make a circle with at least 4" free to do the twisty–windy bit in the next step.

Twist the tails around once (where they cross over each other) – so you have what looks like a twisted wire loop. Now fold the tails back over the ring shape to get the traditional pretzel shape. Tuck the ends underneath & moisten the ends to seal.

Pop your little beauties on a greased cookie sheet & leave them to rise (uncovered) until nice & puffy (20 min).

Preheat your oven to 425°F

Prepare the "dip": bring 2 qts water & ⅓ cup baking soda (not baking powder) to the boil. Very carefully lower a pretzel or two into the water & simmer for 10sec on each side. Lift with a slotted spoon & return them to their cookie sheet.

Brush with the egg white.

- For savory: You can sprinkle coarse salt, poppy or roasted sesame seeds on if you like.

- For sweet: leave them plain & add cinnamon mix after they are baked.

Bake for 4 min, spin the cookie sheet around (so they brown really evenly) & bake for another 4 min. If you are making the sweet variety: dip the newly baked pretzels into melted butter & then into cinnamon sugar & perch them on a rack to cool.

This may seem like a lot of work, but it's really quite simple once you get the hang of it. Enjoy!

English Muffins

These can be frozen. When needed, simply heat in the microwave or toast them.

Serves: 8
Time to Prepare: 3 hrs

Ingredients

- 1 cup Warm Milk
- 3 Tbsp Softened Butter
- 1 Lightly Beaten Egg
- ½ Tsp Salt
- 2 Tsp White Sugar
- 3 cups Flour (All–purpose works fine)
- 1½ Tsp Dry Active Yeast
- Cornmeal for Coating & Scattering over Your Work Area

Directions

Layer the ingredients as per manufacturer recommendations, & start the dough cycle.

Sprinkle some cornmeal over your surface & turn the dough out. Shape it gently into a ½"–thick rectangle & coat the two sides with cornmeal.

Use a wine glass/super large cookie cutter/squeaky–clean (empty) tuna can to get 8–10 rounds cut out.

Pop onto a greased cookie sheet & leave them alone in the warmth until they have almost doubled in volume.

Cooking time: spray a cast–iron griddle with cooking spray & get it heating over a low heat. Dry–fry the muffins for around 5–7 min/side. They should be golden brown.

Split them with a serrated knife & serve warm.

Easy Naan

This can be made ahead of time & frozen

Serves: 4
Time to Prepare: 2 hrs

Ingredients

- ½ cup Warmed Milk
- 2 Tbsp Oil
- ¼ cup Yogurt
- 2 Eggs, Whisked Lightly with a Fork
- 1 Tsp Salt
- 4 cups White or Brown Bread Flour
- 4½ Tsp Instant Yeast (Not dry active, as there is only one rise, so the yeast needs to work fast)

Directions

Grab the bread machine pan & layer the ingredients for the dough as per manufacturer's instructions. Set to the dough cycle for a 2 lb loaf.

Check the dough after 5 min to check the consistency & correct if needed with a Tbsp of either water or flour at a time.

Heat the oven to 450°F & preheat the two (lightly greased) baking sheets you will use.

When the machine is done, turn the dough out onto your floured work surface & punch it down a bit to release some of the built–up gas & divide it into 8 portions. Keep them covered while you work with one piece at a time. Roll each portion out to roughly ¼" thick.

Bake until puffed up (4 min) & then brown the tops under the broiler. Keep the baked bread wrapped in a clean tea–towel to keep them cozy while the rest are being baked.

Panettone Bread

Panettone is essentially the Italian bread version of fruitcake, often made to share with others on special occasions

Serves: 8
Time to Prepare: 5 min

Ingredients

- ¾ cup Lukewarm Water
- ¼ cup Softened (Not melted) Butter
- 2 Lightly Beaten Eggs
- 1½ Tsp Vanilla (Either extract or essence will do)
- 3¼ cups All-purpose Flour
- 2 Tbsp Organic Sugar
- 2 Tbsp Powdered Milk
- 1½ Tsp Salt
- 2 Tsp Dry Active Yeast
- ½ cup Chopped Dried Fruit of Choice (Mixed fruit is tasty)

Directions

Pop all the ingredients (except the dried fruit) into the bread pan in the order recommended by the manufacturer. Set the machine to work on sweet bread with a light crust.

When the machine beeps, add the dried fruit.

Wait for your tasty-smelling prize to cool down before tucking in. Yum.

Bread Machine Challah

A soft, sweet loaf, traditionally braided by Jewish women for special celebrations

Serves: 6
Time to Prepare: 5 min

Ingredients

- ¾ cup Water (Warm)
- 3 Tbsp Soft Margarine
- 3 cups White Bread Flour
- 4 Tbsp Sugar
- 1¼ Tsp Salt
- 2 Tsp Dry Active Yeast
- 1 Egg (2 Small or 1 Large)

Directions

Layer the water, egg, marg, flour, sugar, salt & yeast in the order directed by the manufacturer. Set the machine to a sweet bread cycle (or white bread if you don't have this one on your machine).

After the baking is done, leave the bread in the tin for 10 min before removing it to finish cooling off on a rack.

Cinniraisin Loaf

This is an amazing sweet bread that has cinnamon & raisins in it. You could experiment & use all kinds of fun things like candied citrus peel or even dried pear bits with ginger if you fancy!

Serves: 8
Time to Prepare: 5 min

Ingredients

- 1 cup Warm Water
- 2 Tbsp Soft Marg
- 3 cups White Bread Flour
- 3 Tbsp Sugar
- 1½ Tsp Salt
- 1 Tsp Ground Cinnamon
- 2½ Tsp Dry Active Yeast
- ¾ cup Raisins to Add at the "Beep"

Directions

Layer the ingredients in the bread pan in the order given here: water, marg, flour, sugar, salt, cinnamon & yeast (unless your manufacturer indicates otherwise).

Select the sweet bread setting.

Add the raisins after the initial mix cycle – most machines will beep at this point to let you know it is time to add any interesting stuff like seeds, herbs & the like.

Rosemary Ciabatta

This recipe has two parts & is best made overnight. It is definitely worth the wait! Note: Biga is a type of pre–fermentation used in Italian baking that yields a characteristic texture & flavor. Bread made this way is less perishable.

Serves: 20
Time to Prepare: 30 min

Ingredients

Biga:

- Just Under 1 cup of Lukewarm Water
- 1½ cups White Bread Flour
- ½ Tsp Rapid Rise Yeast

Dough:

- Just Under 1 cup of Lukewarm Water
- ¼ cup Buttermilk
- 2 Tbsp Olive Oil
- 3 cups White Bread Flour
- 1 ½ Tsp Salt
- ½ Tsp Sugar
- ¼ Tsp Dry Active Yeast
- ¼ Tsp Freshly Minced Rosemary (Or a pinch of dried rosemary, crushed)

Directions

Episode One: The Biga the Betta

- Place the Biga ingredients into your bread machine as you would your regular loaf of bread (layer according to manufacturer recommendations). Select the dough cycle & let it knead for 5 minutes or so before switching the machine off. Leave this mix to develop overnight (12–16 hrs)

Episode Two: The Knead to Bake

- Measure out the rest of the ingredients over the biga in the order that works for your machine. Set the machine to work on a basic dough setting.

- Grease two large bowls for the dough to rise in. Once the dough is ready, split it evenly between the bowls & cover with oiled plastic wrap. Set it in a warm spot & wait for it to triple in volume (±1hr).

- Now grab two cookie sheets & dust them with flour. You want to disturb the air bubbles in the dough as little as possible, so work lightly. Shape each lump into a rectangle about 1" in height. Now sprinkle a little flour over them & leave them to rise for the last time: 30 minutes.

- Heat your oven to 425°F & pop the two loaves in for 25–30 minutes. It will be the longest half hour of your life, but be patient.

Tip: If you want a nice crispy crust, you can spray them with water or put a couple of ice cubes in the oven to make steam.

Whole Wheat Buns

Need a healthier variety of bun in your life? Here's the answer to your hamburger troubles. These will keep in the freezer if you seal them in a suitable plastic bag (3–4 weeks). Defrost slowly & give them a quick burst under the broiler to crisp them up.

Serves: 12
Time to Prepare: 5 min

Ingredients

- 1 cup Lukewarm Water
- 1 Lightly Beaten Egg
- 1 cup Whole Wheat Flour
- ¾ Tsp Salt
- ¼ cup Cubed, Softened Butter/Marg
- ¼ cup Sugar
- 3 Tsp Dry Active Yeast
- 1 Tbsp Wheat Gluten (It helps the dough to rise better)
- 2 cups White Flour (Use bread flour if you prefer, then omit the extra gluten)

Directions

Grab your bread machine pan & layer the ingredients as directed by the manufacturer. Get the process going on the dough cycle.

When ready, scoop the dough out of the pan & onto a prepared work surface. Gently shape the dough into a 12" rope.

Find a really sharp knife & separate the rope into either 12 portions for long rolls (hot dog rolls) or into 8 balls for hamburger buns.

Tip: Give the knife a quick spray with cooking spray so the dough doesn't stick.

Spray a cookie sheet with cooking spray & pop the buns/rolls onto it. Pat the buns down a little & gently shape the rolls into roughly 6"–long, hot–dog roll–looking shapes.

Find a warms spot, cover & leave to rise until almost doubled in volume (10–15 min).

Get the oven heating to 400°F & once everything is ready for the big excitement, bake them until golden (10–12 min). Be sure to keep an eye on them.

Pop onto wire racks & devour them once cooled.

Sourdough Bread

Sourdough is the original bread maker's secret. Lovingly crafted from scratch, this little morsel of dough goes a long way.

Serves: 10
Time to Prepare: 15 min

Ingredients

- 1 cup Sourdough Starter (Make your own or purchase some)
- ¾ cup Lukewarm
- 1 Tbsp Sugar
- 3 cups White Bread Flour
- 3 Tbsp Vegetable Oil
- 2 Tsp Salt
- 1 Tbsp Active Dry Yeast (Need a slower paced rise, so instant/rapid rise yeast will just cause It to collapse)

Directions

Many bread machines have a mandatory 20 minute preheat prior to actually mixing. If this is the case, start the machine on a basic bread cycle so long.

Place the sourdough starter with the water, sugar & yeast in the bread pan. Give them a gentle stir. Pop the pan back into the machine & leave the ingredients to meet & greet (10 min). The starter should begin bubbling slightly.

Note: You can do this in the bread machine pan if your manufacturer guidelines recommend putting the wet ingredients in first, if not, remove the starter mix & layer accordingly

Layer the ingredients evenly & select a basic bread cycle, if you have not already done so. About 5 minutes into kneading, check the consistency. If it is too dry or wet, add 1 Tbsp water or flour accordingly.

Ensure you wait until the bread is cool before slicing it or the insides will clump up & the bread will become a torn mass of bits. If you don't really have a problem with presentation, then by all means, tuck in!

Enjoy!

Soft Italian Breadsticks

Serve these as a starter with some fancy soup on a winter's evening

Serves: 8
Time to Prepare: 20 min

Ingredients

Dough:

- 1 cup Warm (Not boiling) Water
- 3 Tbsp Softened Butter
- 1½ Tsp Salt
- 3 cups White Bread Flour
- 2 Tbsp Sugar
- 1 Tsp Italian Seasoning (Or your own blend of herbs)
- 1 Tsp Garlic Powder
- 2¼ Tsp Active Dry Yeast (Not instant)

Topping:

- 1 Tbsp Melted Butter
- 1 Tbsp Grated Parmesan Cheese

Directions

Grab your bread pan & measure all the dough ingredients out into it (use the order specified by the manufacturer), then select the dough cycle.

When the machine is done, turn the dough out onto a lightly floured surface & divide into two portions. Cut each portion in half again (you now have 4 equal lumps).

Roll the portions out & slice into 6 x 5" strips that you will twist & then set on a greased baking sheet. Make sure there is around 2" rise–space between each one. Cover & leave to rise in a warm spot until about double in volume (20 min).

Bake at 350°F until golden brown (15 min), then remove & brush with butter & sprinkle Parmesan over them. If you over–bake the bread sticks, you may wish to pop in your cast–iron dentures before sampling.

Caramelized Onion & Cheese Bread

You can make substitutions here if you like: swap one of the 4 cups of bread flour out for a cup of your fav flour like rye or whole wheat

Serves: 16
Time to Prepare: 30 min

Ingredients

- 1 Tbsp Butter
- 1 Large Onion, Finely Sliced
- 1¼ cups Water
- 1 Tbsp Olive Oil
- 4 cups White Bread Flour
- 2 Tbsp Sugar
- 1 Tsp Salt
- 1½ Tsp Rapid/Instant/Fast Rise Yeast (Or 2 Tsp dry active yeast)

Directions

Fry the onions in butter over a medium heat until brown & caramelized. If you are in too much of a hurry, they will burn instead – this should take 10–15 min.

Pop the rest of the ingredients into the bread pan the way the manufacturer recommends & set it to you most basic cycle with a light crust. Add the onions in at the beep (after about 5 min).

Leave the bread to cool for 20 minutes after it has completed baking.

Tip: If you want to make something that looks fancier than just a plain pan–loaf of bread, set the machine to the dough cycle & add the onions after 5 min. When the dough is ready, turn it out &

shape it however you planned, give it its second rise until double volume, & then bake in a 400°F oven for 30–40 min.

Orange Breakfast Rolls

Not quite orange in color as much as flavor. This favorite is soft, sweet & just perfect for enjoying any time of day.

Serves: 10
Time to Prepare: 1 hr 30 min

Ingredients

- 1½ cups Warm Water
- 4 Tbsp Butter Cubes Softened
- 4 cups Bread Flour
- 1 Tbsp Chopped Candied Orange Rind
- 4 Tbsp Sugar
- 1 Tsp Salt
- 2 Tsp Fast/Instant/Rapid Rise Yeast (or 4 Tsp dry active yeast)
- Coating: ¾ cup Softened Butter
- Orange Sugar: 1 cup of Sugar Mixed with 3 Tbsp Fresh Orange Zest

Directions

Add all the ingredients for the dough into your bread machine in the order recommended by the manufacturer. Select the dough cycle & leave it do its thing.

When it is ready, turn the dough out on a clean & lightly floured surface. Divide into 16 equal balls. Coat the balls with butter & roll them into the orange sugar mix before putting them into 2 x greased 9" pans. Leave them to rise again (30–60 min).

Pop them into your heated oven 350°F until you cannot resist them any longer.

Easy Pizza Dough

A simple & tasty recipe. Make a few batches & freeze them if you like

Serves: 6
Time to Prepare: 3 hrs

Ingredients

- 2 Tsp Dried Yeast
- 3 cups White Bread Flour
- 1 Tsp Salt
- 2 Tbsp Sugar
- 2 Tbsp Oil (Olive)
- 1 "Heaped" cup of Water (i.e. Just more than a cup)
- 2 Tbsp Water

Directions

Layer the ingredients in your bread pan (use the order specified by the manufacturer) & select the dough cycle.

Once complete, you will pop it into a well–greased bowl & leave it to rise in a warm spot until it looks voluptuous again (30 min). Try not to handle it too much.

Roll the dough into the desired shape (square pizza is perfectly edible), add toppings & bake at 225°F until the cheese is all bubbly & smells good (roughly 10 min).

If you are a fan of thin–based, crispy pizzas, bake the dough first (before adding the toppings), then continue as usual with toppings etc.

Suggestions:

- 4 Cheeses: Mozzarella, Camembert, Romano & Feta

- Try adding caramelized onions and/or roasted garlic to your fav toppings

- 50/50 mix of basil pesto & olive oil with a hard cheese like Parmesan

- Ooh–la–la: Cranberry jelly with some shredded (leftover?) chicken & sliced Brie

- Speaking of Which: Combine Mozzarella, your meat of choice (eg shredded chicken), & sliced avocado.

- Don't forget about the semi–dried tomatoes (too dry & you can't eat/slice it) & sliced olives

- Season to taste with salt & pepper & herbs of choice

Calzone

Calzone is traditionally a folded pizza with all kinds of yumminess inside

Serves: 8
Time to Prepare: 20 min

Ingredients

- 1¼ cups Warm Water
- 1 Tsp Table Salt
- ½ Tsp Dried Oregano
- ½ Tsp Dried Basil
- ½ Tsp Garlic Powder
- 3 cups White Bread Flour
- 1 Tsp Powdered Milk
- 1½ Tbsp Sugar
- 2 Tsp Yeast (Active dry)
- ¾ cup Your Favorite Pizza Sauce
- 4 oz Pepperoni (Or similar), Chopped
- 2 Tbsp Melted Butter
- 1¼ cups Grated Mozzarella Cheese (More if you like things "properly" cheesed)

Directions

Layer the ingredients (water, herbs & seasoning, flour, milk powder, sugar, & yeast) in the order recommended by the manufacturer & select the dough cycle.

Get your oven heating to 350°F.

When the dough is ready, roll it out thinly. Draw an imaginary line down the center & spread the pizza sauce, cheese, & pepperoni in the first half. Fold the other half over the top & seal the edges well with water. Brush the top with melted butter. Bake for 35–45 min.

Fancy Variation:

- When the dough is done, roll it out onto a surface that is clean & dusted with flour. Shape it into a 10x16" rectangle & pop it onto a greased cookie sheet.

- Paint a stripe down the middle with the pizza sauce & sprinkle the cheese & pepperoni on top of the stripe. The empty space on either side of the stripe will laced together over the top.

- Cut the "lacing–slits" on each side of the rectangle, roughly 1–1½" apart & about ½" away from the filling. Now take each little piece & lace it over its friend on the other side of the filling: kind of like crossing your arms, one piece goes under, the other over. Pinch the ends of each lace & give it a little twist as you do so to finish off neatly. Seal with water as you go & finally brush the top with the melted butter before baking (35–45 min at 350°F).

Creamy Rye

Rye bread has a special place in the hearts of many a bread–lover. Not only is it lower on the glycemic index & generally considered healthier for you, but it has a unique & wonderful deep flavor.

Serves: 4
Time to Prepare: 1 hr 30 min

Ingredients

* A Little Less Than 1 cup Warm Water
* 2½ cups Bread Flour
* 1 ½ Tsp Table Salt
* 2 Tbsp Softened Butter
* 2 Tbsp Sticky Brown Sugar
* ¾ cup Rye Flour
* 1½ Tsp Cocoa Powder
* ½ cup Sour Cream
* 1 ½ Tbsp Natural Molasses
* 1 & a Pinch Tsp Instant Yeast or 2 Tsp Active Dry Yeast
* 2 Tsp Caraway Seeds (Can use anise seeds for a slightly different flavor)

Directions

Layer the ingredients as directed by the manufacturer & set onto the regular old bread cycle to bake.

If you are using instant yeast, you could also use the rapid cycle, but it will yield a texture that is slightly coarser

The Classic Bagel

For an egg–free version, sub the egg wash out for a quick spray of non–stick coating. Make your bagels interesting by sprinkling some seeds on the top before baking.

Serves: 10
Time to Prepare: 1 hr 30 min

Ingredients

- 1 ¼ cups Warm Water
- 3 cups Bread Flour
- 3⅓ Tbsp Organic Brown Sugar
- 1 Tsp Salt
- 2½ Tsp Fast/Instant/Rapid Rise Yeast (Or 3¼ Tsp active dry yeast)
- Boiling Water Dip: 3 Qt Water with 1 Tbsp Sugar
- Egg Wash: 1 Egg Mixed with 1 Tbsp Water

Directions

Pop all the ingredients (except the egg wash) into your machine as recommended by the manufacturer. Get the dough cycle going & make yourself some coffee while you contemplate the marvels of modern cooking.

Turn the dough out onto a lightly floured work space & separate it into 8 equal balls. Work delicately while you gently press your thumb through the center & stretch it into as close to a bagel shape as you can get. Leave them to do their second rise in a warm spot.

Start heating your oven to 400°F .

Boil the water for the dip (3qt water, 1 Tbsp sugar) & carefully lower each bagel with a slotted spoon. Boil on each side for 1½ min, then cool them on a rack for a minute (literally) before doing the egg wash. Pop them onto a greased cookie sheet & sprinkle some seeds on at this point if you like.

Bake until golden (15 min) & blush with pride.

Variations:

- Bagel sticks (simply make sticks, not rings) can be rolled in a sesame–poppy mix with a pinch of garlic powder before baking.

- Bagel chips can be made with leftover bagels (if there was such a thing). Simply slice them thinly & spread the mini–disks with butter. Lay them butter–side up on a cookie sheet & bake until golden (12–15 min) in a 375° oven

Whole Wheat Apple & Cinnamon Bread

This is a must try recipe – as easy as pie

Serves: 10
Time to Prepare: 10 min

Ingredients

- 1⅓ cups 100% Natural Apple Juice
- 1 Tbsp Raw Honey
- 1½ Tsp Salt
- 1 Tsp Ground Cinnamon
- ⅓ cup Grated/Chopped Apple
- ¼ cup Wheat Gluten (¼ Tsp guar can be used instead)
- 3¼ cups Whole Wheat Flour
- ½ cup Plain Breakfast Oats
- 3 Tsp Dry Active Yeast
- 2 Tbsp Orange Juice Concentrate (Or 2 Tsp of citrus marmalade mixed with 2 Tbsp water)

Directions

Layer the ingredients in the bread pan as directed by the manufacturer. Set the machine to whole wheat for a 1½ lb loaf & leave it to run its course.

Leave to cool before slicing it.

This is the most amazing stuff to toast for breakfast & enjoy together with a cup of fresh coffee & a Sudoku puzzle. You don't eat the puzzle, though

Doughnuts

No bread machine has quite served its purpose until it has at least made one batch of doughnuts. Make this with little people & watch them buzz with excitement – just watch they stay far away from the hot oil.

Serves: 12
Time to Prepare: 15 min

Ingredients

- 1¼ cups Warmed Milk
- 1 Lightly Mixed Egg
- ¼ cup Softened Butter/Marg
- ¼ cup White Sugar
- 1 Tsp Salt
- 3½ cups All–purpose Flour
- 1½ Tsp Dry Active Yeast

Directions

Layer the ingredients in the bread pan as directed by the manufacturer, select the dough setting & leave the machine to do its thing.

When the dough is ready, roll it out on your prepared work surface to about ½" thick. If you have a doughnut cutter (2½"), use that. Otherwise, you can use a large cookie–cutter & a juice bottle cap to get the center hole out. Some people prefer to make square doughnuts with a little slit cut in the center for the oil to get through. Less dough wasted this way...

Either way, leave your round/square treats to rise in a warm spot until doubled (approximately 30 min). Then deep–fry in hot oil (375°F). Turn them as they rise to the surface so that they are beautifully golden on both sides. Drain on paper towels & dust immediately with sugar – or, once cooled, you can put frosting or chocolate on them.

Have fun!

Sage & Onion Bread

These flavors blend especially well with leftover roast chicken. Just saying.

Serves: 12
Time to Prepare: 10 min

Ingredients

- 1 cup Lukewarm Water, with a Little Bit to Spare for Adjustments
- 1 Small Onion Coarsely Chopped Onion (⅓ cup)
- 2 Tbsp Softened Butter
- 2½ cups Bread Flour
- 1 cup Whole Wheat Flour
- 1 Tbsp Sugar
- 1 Tsp Salt
- 2 Tsp Dry Active Yeast
- 1¾ Tsp Dry Sage (Rub it between hands to release flavors)

Directions

Layer the ingredients in the bread pan as per manufacturer's instructions. Select the whole wheat cycle (this has a longer rise time than plain white bread).

About 5–10 minutes in, check the consistency & add either water or flour, 1 Tbsp at a time if it needs adjusting. The dough should be tacky & sticky but when you roll it into a ball between your fingers it should not stick to your fingers.

Leave the machine to work its magic. Usually, machines take around 3 hours to bake whole wheat bread but your machine will give you the exact time.

Leave the bread to cool for an hour before slicing, so mentally add that hour to the bake time. One hour of merely looking at a loaf of fresh bread can be mentally exhausting.

Moravian Sugar Cake

This is a cake that is rich, sweet & extremely delicious. It makes an excellent coffee cake any time of year.

Serves: 8
Time to Prepare: 30 min

Ingredients

- ⅝ cup Water
- 2 Eggs, Lightly Mixed with a Fork
- 3 cups Flour (General all–purpose flour)
- 1 Tsp Salt
- ½ cup Softened Butter
- ½ cup Sugar
- 1 Tsp Vanilla/Essence Extract
- 2 Tsp Rapid Rise/instant Yeast
- ½ cup Dry Instant Mashed Potato (No flavored package – save that for a savory variation experiment)

Yummy Stuff for the Top:

- ½ cup Melted Butter
- Frosting: ¾ cup Icing Sugar Mixed with ±4 Tsp Milk
- Cinnamon Sugar Mix: 1 cup Light Brown Sugar + 2 Tsp Cinnamon

Directions

Check the user guide for your machine & add the ingredients in the order recommended by the manufacturer. Select the dough setting & leave the machine to do its thing.

Grease a 16x12x1" baking pan (or a 15x10x1" jelly roll pan).

When the dough is ready, turn it out into the pan & gently stretch & press it to fit evenly. Cover & leave it to rise until doubled in volume (30–45 min).

Heat the oven 350°F.

Meantime, make up the cinnamon sugar in a little dish. When the dough is done, use two fingers to poke deep holes all over. Then sprinkle the sugar mix evenly over everything before drizzling the melted butter over the top. Bake until golden (20–25 min)

When it is cooked, place it onto a serving platter & serve warm with or without the frosting drizzled over the top.

Cheddar Bread

Bread & cheese are classic companions. Why not bake the bread with the cheese already inside?

Serves: 8
Time to Prepare: 10 min

Ingredients

- 1 Package of Yeast
- 3 cups White Bread Flour
- ¼ cup Low–fat Milk Powder
- 1 Tbsp Softened Butter
- 1 Tsp Salt
- 2 Tbsp White Sugar
- 1¼ cups Warmed Water
- 1½ cups Shredded Cheese: Sharp Cheddar Works Well
- ⅓ cup Freshly Grated Parmesan
- 1 Tsp Freshly Ground Black Peppercorns

Directions

Follow the instructions for layering the ingredients given by the machine manufacturer.

Add the cheeses & pepper either at the beginning of the cycle with the dough ingredients or at the beep stage when the machine says it is time to add extras in.

Select the white bread setting for 1½ lb loaf. Leave to cool slightly before turning the bread out of the pan

Sweet Hawaiian Yeast Bread

Here's one you can make to impress your friends; it is a little different to the standard sandwich loaf

Serves: 12
Time to Prepare: 5 min

Ingredients

- ¾ cup Pineapple Juice – Heated
- 1 Egg, Lightly Mixed
- 2 Tbsp Oil
- 2½ Tbsp Organic Honey
- ¾ Tsp Salt
- 3 cups White Bread Flour
- 2 Tbsp Full–fat Milk Powder
- 2 Tsp Fast/Quick/Rapid/Instant Yeast

Directions

Get the ingredients into the pan in the order recommended by the manufacturer, keeping the liquids & yeast at opposite ends of the flour barrier.

Set the cycle to sweet bread (or white) & make sure that you have selected a light crust.

Leave to cool in the pan for a few minutes before tipping the bread out.

Multigrain Health Bread

Need to impress your health–nut friend? Give this one a try.
Not recommended for baking with the time delay feature.

Serves: 12
Time to Prepare: 5 min

Ingredients

- ¼ cup Lukewarm Water
- 1 Egg, Beaten Slightly
- ½ cup Plain Yogurt
- 2 Tbsp Canola Oil
- 3 Tbsp Organic Brown Sugar
- 1½ Tsp Salt
- ¼ cup Rolled/Quick–cooking Oats
- ¼ cup Bran
- 1 cup General All–purpose White Flour
- 1½ cups Whole Wheat Flour
- 2¼ Tsp Active Dry Yeast

Directions

Refer to the manufacturer's instructions & layer the ingredients accordingly. Set the cycle to 1½ lb whole wheat & check the consistency after around 5–10 min of kneading.

Add 1 Tbsp of either water or flour to adjust if necessary. Check by making a little ball between your fingers: it should be tacky but not sticky.

Tomato Bread

Here is a beautifully seasoned bread with a difference. Eat this bread with fresh mozzarella & basil leaves.

Serves: 8
Time to Prepare: 10 min

Ingredients

* ¼–⅜ cup Lukewarm Milk
* 6 Tbsp Tomato Paste
* 1 Egg, Broken Up with a Fork
* 2 Tsp Oil (Canola or olive)
* ½ Tsp Salt
* 2 Tsp Sugar
* 2 cups White Bread Flour
* 1½ Tsp Dried Onion Flakes (Or 1 Tsp onion powder)
* ¼ Tsp Garlic Powder
* ¼ Tsp Ground Nutmeg
* 1–1½ Tsp Dry Active Yeast
* ½ Tsp Italian Seasoning (Or your own herb blend that includes rosemary & basil)

Directions

If your machine manufacturer recommends layering the ingredients from wet to dry: then add them in the order listed here. Otherwise, follow the instructions that came with your machine.

Set the cycle on your regular, basic bread setting for a 1 lb loaf with a light crust. Leave it to do its thing & leave it to cool completely before slicing (20–60min).

Enjoy the fruits of your labor with some good butter.

Cinnabuns

Who can resist a cinnamon bun?
Make them yourself & share them as gifts

Serves: 12
Time to Prepare: 10 min

Ingredients

Basic Bun:

- 1 cup Warmed Milk
- 3 Tbsp Water
- 1 Beaten Egg
- ¼ cup Soft Butter
- 3⅓ cups White Flour (Just regular old cake flour)
- 3 Tbsp Sugar
- ¾ Tsp Salt
- 2 Tsp Dry Active Yeast

Filling:

- ¾ cup Sticky Brown Sugar (Packed)
- 3¾ Tsp Cinnamon – or More if You Love Cinnamon
- 2 Tbsp Softened Butter/Marg

Glaze:

- ¾ cup Icing Sugar
- ¼ Tsp Vanilla Essence
- 2–3 Tsp Milk

Directions

Put the ingredients into the bread pan as per manufacturer's instructions. Some put the yeast in first, then the flour, sugar &

salt, then the butter, milk, egg, & water, others in the reverse order. Either way – make sure the yeast & liquids are at opposite ends.

Set the machine to work on the dough cycle & when done, turn the dough out onto a lightly floured work surface. If it is too sticky, add a little flour to make it easier to handle & leave it to sit for 10 minutes or so.

Roll out into a large rectangle roughly ¼" thick. Spread the filling out over it & roll it up. Cut 1"–thick slices (use a very sharp knife to avoid squashing the roll) & pop them onto a greased, 9x13" baking pan.

Now cover & leave to process in the spot the cat normally picks (make sure the cat is in another room). After roughly 30 min, the dough should have doubled in volume.

Get the oven to 350° & bake until lightly golden on top (25 min). When they are out the oven & cool enough, make a glaze swirl over the tops of the buns. Yummy.

Pumpernickel

Pumpernickel is a sweet & heavy rye bread that has an interesting history. If you ever have the time to investigate, this makes for a highly amusing tidbit to share are your next meal. Or not.... Let's just say that this bread wasn't always so tasty, & that many endured intestinal discomfort after eating it

Serves: 16
Time to Prepare: 10 min

Ingredients

- 1⅛ cups Lukewarm Water
- ⅓ cup Natural Molasses
- 1 ½ Tbsp Oil
- 1½ cups White Bread Flour
- 1 cup Rye Flour
- 1 cup Whole Wheat Flour
- 1½ Tsp Salt
- 3 Tbsp Cocoa Powder (Unsweetened)
- 2 Tsp Dry Active Yeast
- 1 ½ Tbsp Caraway Seeds (Can be substituted with anise seed for a different result)

Directions

Layer all the ingredients as recommended by the manufacturer. Set the machine to basic bread, 1½ lb, with a light crust. After about 5 minutes of kneading, check if the dough needs adjustment. 1 Tbsp of either warm water or flour at a time.

Tip: You know the dough is right when you pinch a piece off & you are able to roll it into a ball easily. It should be a little tacky still.

Remember to leave the loaf to cool after baking before you tuck into it. This is very hard, so lock yourself out the kitchen for 20 minutes or so.

Russian Black Bread

Very similar to the Germanic Pumpernickel which has a meaning rooted deeply in humor. This Russian version not only has a better name, but has a little something extra in it that makes it unique.

Serves: 12
Time to Prepare: 10 min

Ingredients

- 1½ cups Lukewarm Water
- 2 Tbsp Cloudy Apple Cider Vinegar
- 2 ½ cups White Bread Flour
- 1 cup Organic Rye Flour
- 1 Tsp Salt
- 2 Tbsp Butter/Marg
- 2 Tbsp Sweet Molasses (Dark corn syrup will also do)
- 1 Tbsp Sticky Brown Sugar
- 3 Tbsp Cocoa Powder (Check that it is unsweetened)
- 1 Tsp Instant Coffee Powder
- 1 Tbsp Caraway Seeds
- 2 Tsp Dry Active Yeast

Directions

Measure out & layer all the ingredients in the order recommended by the manufacturer. Set the machine to whole wheat with a medium crust.

When the machine is done, leave it to cool completely on a rack before slicing.

Banana Nut Bread

Feel free to experiment here. Have fun substituting the nuts for choc chips, raisins, perhaps even sunflower or pumpkin seeds.

Serves: 8
Time to Prepare: 1 hr

Ingredients

- 1½ cups Flour
- ⅔ cup Sugar
- 1 Tsp Baking Powder
- ½ Tsp Bicarbonate of Soda (Baking soda)
- ½ Tsp Salt
- ⅓ cup Oil
- 2 XL Eggs (3 large), Beaten Lightly
- ¼ cup Sour Cream
- 1 Tsp Vanilla Essence
- ⅔ cup Mashed Ripe Banana
- ⅓ Finely Chopped Nuts of Choice (Pecan and/or walnut)

Directions

Add the ingredients in the order your machine manufacturer directs. You will layer everything except the banana & nuts – those you will add later.

Select the setting for cake & start the machine. Don't forget to add the banana & nuts at the beep (after around 5 minutes).

When the baking is done, carefully lift the pan out the machine & turn the bread out onto a cooling rack. Make sure the bread is cold before slicing it – otherwise you will have a tasty mess to serve

Classic Hamburger Buns

Nothing could be nicer than an evening making burgers & eating them on homemade buns

Serves: 12
Time to Prepare: 10 min

Ingredients

- 1¼ Warmed cups Milk
- 1 Lightly Beaten Egg
- 2 Tbsp Butter/Oil
- ¼ cup Sugar
- ¾ Tsp Salt
- 3 ¾ cups White Bread Flour
- 1 ¼ Tsp Active Dry Yeast (Not instant – there is a difference)

Directions

Pop all the ingredients– except the butter – into the bread pan (use the order specified by the manufacturer) & set the machine to run a dough cycle.

When the dough is ready, turn it out onto a lightly floured surface & shape into 12 rolls, roughly 1" thick. Set on a greased cookie sheet & give them a quick brush with melted butter. Leave in a warm spot until doubled (about an hour).

Get your oven to 350°F & bake until done to your liking. If you have a fan–assisted oven, you may have food ready to eat in 10 minutes. Otherwlse, if you are using a regular oven, check to see if they are done after 20 minutes or so.

Tip: To get neat & tidy buns, roll it out flat & use a glass (greased) that has a wide enough mouth (roughly 3½" wide) as a cookie–cutter.

Sweet Cinnamon Bread

Makes a 1½ lb loaf of happiness

Serves: 6
Time to Prepare: 10 min

Ingredients

- 1 cup Milk, Warmed
- ¼ cup Soft Butter/Marg
- 1 Lightly Beaten Egg
- 3 cups White Bread Flour
- ½ cup Table Sugar
- ½ Tsp Salt
- 1¼ Tsp Ground Cinnamon
- 2 Tsp Dry Active Yeast

Directions

Layer the ingredients as per manufacturer guidelines & bake using the sweet bread setting (or just use the white bread one).

Check the dough after about 5 minutes & adjust the consistency with flour or water as needed. When the bread is done, leave it to sit for 10 minutes or so before turning it out. You may need to loosen it slightly with a spatula.

Make a schedule & stick to who gets to eat the fresh crust this time…

Pita Bread

The ultimate sandwich. Pita bread dates back at least 12 000 years to somewhere in the middle "yeast". The possibilities are endless here.

Serves: 10
Time to Prepare: 5 min

Ingredients

- 1 ⅓ cups Warm (Not boiling) Water
- 2 Tbsp Oil (Canola or olive)
- 1 Tbsp Organic Sugar
- 1¼ Tsp Salt
- 2 cups White All–purpose Flour
- 2½ Tsp Dry Active Yeast
- 1⅓ cups Whole Wheat Flour (Crushed wheat is ok, but can be a nuisance for some sets of teeth)

Directions

Layer all the ingredients in your bread pan as per manufacturer's instructions & set the machine to dough (manual).

When the dough is done, divide it into 10 equal balls & pop them onto prepared cookie sheet(s). Leave them to bask in a warm spot for around 20 min & get your oven heating to 500°F.

Before popping the puffed up balls into the oven, play pat–a–cake & flatten them into a roughly 6" disk.

Note: The second rise should not be totally "complete" because you want that last little bit of yeast development to give you the hollow pocket.

Bake for 5 min. The tops should poof out a bit & go brown... And there you go. Cut each one in half & stuff with your fav fillings

Caramelized Onion Focaccia

Focaccia is typically a flat, oven–baked bread, similar to a pizza in nature. You can adjust the toppings freely, so have fun with this concept.

Serves: 4
Time to Prepare: 50 min

Ingredients

* ¾ cup Lukewarm Water
* 2 Tbsp Vegetable Oil
* 1 Tbsp Sugar
* 1 Tsp Salt
* 2 cups White Bread Flour
* 1½ Tsp Dry Active Yeast
* ¾ cup Grated Mozzarella Cheese
* 2 Tbsp Grated Parmesan Cheese
* Onion Topping
* 3 Tbsp Soft Butter
* 2 Medium Onions Finely Chopped
* 2 Minced Cloves of Garlic

Directions

Measure out & layer the water, oil, sugar, salt, flour, yeast as directed by your machine's manufacturer. Set the program to "dough" & let the machine do its work.

When the dough is ready, turn it out onto a lightly floured large cookie sheet & pat it into a 12" circle. Leave it to rise (covered) until almost double in volume (±30 min)

Meanwhile, fry the onions & garlic in butter (very gently: med–low heat) until the onion is just right.

Set the oven to 400°F.

Fetch the dough when it is ready & make a bunch of holes all over (roughly 1" apart) with the handle of a wooden spoon. Now spread the tasty topping over the dough, scatter the mozzarella & parmesan over that & voila! it is ready for baking.

Bake until the edge is golden (15–20 min).

Leave to cool for a few minutes before cutting the bread into wedges like a pizza.

100% Whole Wheat Brown Bread

Baking whole wheat breads is generally not recommended as a starting point in the journey of bread making, but with a bread machine, this becomes way easier. Just bear in mind the type of yeast you use here could make or break your loaf.

Serves: 12
Time to Prepare: 10 mins

Ingredients

- 1 ½ cups Warm (Not boiling) Water
- 2 Tbsp Dry Milk Powder
- 2 Tbsp Marg/Butter
- 2 Tbsp Raw Honey
- 2 Tbsp Black Molasses
- 1½ Tsp Salt
- 3⅓ cups Whole Wheat Bread Flour
- 1 ½ Tsp Yeast

Directions

Layer the ingredients as instructed by the manufacturer of your machine, & set the cycle on whole wheat for a 2 lb loaf.

When the machine is done & you are drooling uncontrollably at the thought of some tasty bread, leave the bread in the pan (but out the machine) for 20 min before cutting it.

Brioche

Brioche is a sweet bread of French origin. It has a higher egg & butter content than other breads which gives it a beautifully rich & tender crumb.

Serves: 6
Time to Prepare: 10 min

Ingredients

- 1¾ Tsp Dry Active Yeast
- 1¾ cups White Bread Flour
- 2 Tbsp Extra Bread Flour
- 3 Tbsp White Sugar
- ¾ Tsp Salt
- 2 Whole Eggs, Lightly Beaten
- 1 Egg Yolk
- ¼ cup Warm Water
- 2 Tbsp Extra Water
- 8 Tbsp Butter (Purists will tell you to use unsalted, but any butter will do just fine)

Directions

Layer the ingredients (except the butter) in your bread pan as per manufacturer's instructions & set to the basic bread cycle.

Cut the butter up into little blocks & add them in one Tsp every minute around 10 min before the end of the first kneading cycle. Set this time aside to drink some tea & contemplate the dishes, but DO NOT RUSH.

Leave the machine to do its thing & when the bread is done, open the machine & leave it to cool in its pan for around 20 min. This will give it time to firm up (i.e. keep the sides from going wonky).

Italian Country Bread

This is a wonderful flatbread. It is economical & filling. Definitely a keeper!

Serves: 2
Time to Prepare: 2 hr 30 min

Ingredients

- ¾ cup Warm Water
- 2 Tbsp Oil (Olive)
- 2 cups Flour
- 1 Tbsp Salt
- 1½ Tbsp White Sugar
- 1 Tbsp Dry Active Yeast
- Rosemary & Salt to Garnish
- 1½ Tbsp Dried Rosemary, Crushed Lightly in Your Hand to Release the Fragrance a Bit

Directions

Layer the ingredients in the order specified by the manufacturer, & set it on the dough cycle.

Once complete, lump the dough out onto a greased baking sheet & shape it by hand into a thin (1"?) layer. Cover it & leave it to do its thing until doubled in volume (anywhere from 30 min to 1 hr).

Get your oven heating to 375°F.

Brush the bread lightly with olive oil & sprinkle with salt & rosemary, then bake until golden & crisp (20–25 min).

Leave the bread intact when serving, so everyone can tear pieces off savagely for themselves.

Stuffed Focaccia

Again, a very versatile concept that could incorporate any combination of herbs

Serves: 8
Time to Prepare: 20 min

Ingredients

- 1 Tbsp Dry Active Yeast
- 3 cups Bread Flour
- 1½ Tsp Salt
- 1 Tsp Freshly Ground Black Pepper
- 1 Tsp Dried Rosemary (1 Tbsp if using freshly chopped)
- ¼ cup Olive Oil
- 1¼ cups Lukewarm Water

Filling & Topping:

- ½ cup Soft Sun–dried Tomatoes, Cut into Bits – Keep the Oil
- 4 oz Cream/Goats Cheese
- 2 Tbsp Oil from the Sun–dried Tomatoes
- Coarse Salt
- ⅓ cup Oil–cured Halved Black Olives – Keep the Oil for the Last Step

Directions

Layer all the dough ingredients into your bread machine pan. Refer to the manufacturer's instructions for the order in which you should add them. Set the cycle to manual/dough. After roughly 5 minutes, check the dough to see if it needs adjusting. Use either 1 Tbsp of either water or flour at a time.

When the machine is done with its work, turn it out onto a floured work surface & knead it a few times. Cover with a clean cloth while you prepare the toppings.

Grab a 10" springform pan & grease it lightly.

Cut the dough in half & stretch each one of the halves into a circle big enough to fit in the bottom of the pan.

Scatter the filling ingredients (tomatoes, olives, bits of cream cheese) over the dough. Make sure there is a clear 1" rim around the edge of the dough. Moisten this edge a little with water & carefully lay the other dough circle on top. Pinch the edges together to seal.

Get the sharpest knife you have & slice 3 x ½"–long slits in the top layer. Cover the pan with cling wrap (or an UNUSED disposable shower cap) & leave it in a warm spot to rise until doubled in volume. (± 30 min).

Heat the oven to 475°F.

Use your fingertips to make a few depressions in the top layer & drizzle a little oil from the sun–dried tomatoes & olives over it. Sprinkle salt generously.

Bake until the top is golden (20–25 min). Release the springform sides & allow to cool for at least 10 min before cutting it open.

Enjoy!

Sour Cream Chive Bread

This recipe uses sour cream – so the use of your machine's time–delay is not recommended

Serves: 8
Time to Prepare: 10 min

Ingredients

- ⅔ cup Lukewarm Milk
- ¼ cup Lukewarm Water
- ¼ cup Sour Cream
- 2 Tbsp Butter/Marg
- 1½ Tsp Sugar
- 1½ Tsp Salt
- 3 cups White Bread Flour
- ⅛ Tsp Baking Soda (Not Baking Powder)
- ¼ cup Minced Chives
- 2¼ Tsp Active Dry Yeast

Directions

Layer all the ingredients in your bread pan as recommended by the manufacturer & select the basic bread (or white bread) setting. The loaf size will be 1½ lb.

Check the dough after the beep to see if it needs adjusting: either a Tbsp water or flour to help it.

Leave the machine to do its work, but remember to leave the bread to cool before slicing it (20 min).

Basic Dinner Rolls

This is your go-to recipe for basic bread making. It's a good place to become comfortable with the process.

Serves: 15
Time to Prepare: 30 min

Ingredients

- 1 cup Warm Water, Plus a Little More if Necessary
- 1 Tbsp Water
- 1 Large Egg
- 4½ Tsp Oil
- 3¼ cups White Bread Flour
- ¼ cup Organic, Raw or Table Sugar
- 1½ Tsp Salt
- 2¼ Tsp Instant Yeast (Packaging must say "instant")
- 2 Tbsp Melted Butter

Directions

Grab the bread machine pan & get the ingredients in (use the order specified by the manufacturer), except the butter & shortening (water, egg, oil, flour, sugar, salt, yeast).

Pick the most basic setting your machine has (or simply the dough cycle if you intend to make to make rolls).

Check back after 5 min & add a tablespoon or so of either flour or water to correct the consistency.

Grease a baking sheet (9x13" works well) & shape the dough into 15 little rolls. Brush lightly with a little oil/melted butter. Find a cozy spot, cover & leave to rise until roughly doubled in volume.

Heat the oven to 350°F & bake until golden (12–15min). Brush the tops again with butter after you take them out. After removing from the oven, brush the tops of the rolls with melted butter.

The Herb Garden Bread

Have a surplus of herb lying around going to waste? Snap them up for this tasty & fresh variation on a standard loaf of bread

Serves: 12
Time to Prepare: 2 hrs

Ingredients

- 1¼ cups Lukewarm Water
- 2 Tbsp Butter
- 3 cups Bread Flour
- 2 Tbsp Milk Powder
- 2 Tbsp Sugar
- 1½ Tsp Salt
- 2 Tsp Chives
- 2 Tsp Dried Marjoram (2 Tbsp of freshly chopped)
- 2 Tsp Dried Thyme (2 Tbsp of freshly chopped)
- 1 Tsp Dried Basil (1 Tbsp freshly chopped)
- 1 ½ Tsp Fast Rise Yeast or 2 Tsp Active Dry Yeast

Directions

Layer the ingredients in your bread pan as per instructions that came with your machine. Set it to work on either the white bread or rapid cycle.

Variation:

- Rosemary Bread: Use 1 Tsp dried marjoram & 1 Tsp thyme. Replace the chives & basil with freshly chopped rosemary. Feel free to experiment with herbs & spices.

Beetroot Bread

Here is the healthy version of red velvet cakes. Ok maybe not so much, but still really tasty & definitely worth a try!

Serves: 8
Time to Prepare: 15 min

Ingredients

- ⅔ cup Tepid Water
- 1 cup Grated Beetroot (Raw)
- 3¼ cups Bread Flour
- 1 Tbsp Softened Butter
- 1½ Tsp Salt
- 1 Tsp Organic Sugar
- 1 Tsp Dry Active Yeast

Directions

Check the manual that came with your bread machine for the correct layering of ingredients. Pop all the ingredients is & set the machine to basic white with a medium crust.

Check about 5 minutes into the kneading cycle that everything is A–ok. Adjust with 1 Tbsp water or flour at a time to get the right consistency.

When the machine is done, leave the loaf to cool on a wire rack before slicing it.

Hoagie Rolls

The hoagie roll is used to make the famous Philly Cheesesteak Sandwich. Legend has it that the name hoagie hails from World War 1 as the sandwich from Hog Island, Philadelphia.

Serves: 6
Time to Prepare: 10 min

Ingredients

- 1 cup Lukewarm Water
- 2 Tsp Sugar
- 4 Tsp Canola Oil
- 1 Tsp Salt
- 2¾ cups Flour (White bread flour or plain old all–purpose flour)
- 2¼ Tsp Rapid/Fast/Instant Rise Yeast

Directions

Pop the ingredients into the bread pan in the order recommended by the manufacturer. Set the cycle to "dough".

Turn the dough out onto a lightly floured surface & give it a punch (not the drink) & form it into a loaf. Sprinkle a little flour over the top & smooth it over.

Find a very sharp knife & cut into 6 equal pieces. Shape them lightly into ovalish–rectangles & then space out evenly on a greased cookie sheet. Grab your scissors & give each one a little snip on the top–center of the roll: about ¼" deep & 2" long.

Cover & leave to rise in a cozy spot away from any curious animals & children. Once they look nice & fat, pop them into a preheated 400°F oven until they look tasty (20–25 min).

Tip: Grease your hands a bit before working with the dough. Use butter, a drop of oil or just spray them with cooking spray. The knife can be greased likewise for a nice clean cut.

64469233R00047

Made in the USA
Lexington, KY
09 June 2017